The Shaft

CHARLES TOMLINSON

The Shaft

1978

OXFORD UNIVERSITY PRESS

OXFORD   LONDON   NEW YORK

Oxford University Press, Walton Street, Oxford OX2 6DP

OXFORD LONDON GLASGOW NEW YORK
TORONTO MELBOURNE WELLINGTON CAPE TOWN
IBADAN NAIROBI DAR ES SALAAM
KUALA LUMPUR SINGAPORE JAKARTA HONG KONG TOKYO
DELHI BOMBAY CALCUTTA MADRAS KARACHI

© *Charles Tomlinson 1978*

British Library Cataloguing in Publication Data

Tomlinson, Charles
  The shaft.
  I. Title
  821'.9'14   PR6039.0349S/   77–30650
  ISBN 0–19–211881–1

PRINTED IN GREAT BRITAIN BY
THE BOWERING PRESS LTD,
PLYMOUTH

TO JUSTINE AND JULIET

CONTENTS

I HISTORIES

II PERFECTIONS

III SEASONS

IV BAGATELLES

V IN ARDEN

ACKNOWLEDGEMENTS

Acknowledgements are due to the editors of the following anthologies and periodicals in which some of these poems first appeared :
The Christian Science Monitor, The Hudson Review, The Iowa Review, New Poems 1976–77 (P.E.N.), *New Poetry 2* (Arts Council), *The Ouzel, Poetry Dimension, Poetry Nation, Poetry Nation Review, Poetry Supplement* (The Poetry Book Society), *Stand, The Sunday Telegraph, The Times Literary Supplement.*

I must also thank the producers of 'Poetry Now' and 'Westward Look' (B.B.C.), the Arts Council for an award, the Cheltenham Festival for a poetry prize, and the Shakespeare Birthplace Trust for commissioning 'In Arden'.

I HISTORIES

CHARLOTTE CORDAY

O Vertu! le poignard, seul espoir de la terre,
Est ton arme sacrée . . . .

Chénier

Courteously self-assured, although alone,
With voice and features that could do no hurt,
Why should she not enter? They let in
A girl whose reading made a heroine—
Her book was Plutarch, her republic Rome :
Home was where she sought her tyrant out.

The towelled head next, the huge batrachian mouth :
There was a mildness in him, even. He
Had never been a woman's enemy,
And time and sickness turned his stomach now
From random execution. All the same,
He moved aside to write her victims down,
And when she approached, it was to kill she came.

She struck him from above. One thrust. Her whole
Intent and innocence directing it
To breach through flesh and enter where it must,
It seemed a blow that rose up from within :
Tinville reduced it all to expertise :
—What, would you make of me a hired assassin?

—What did you find to hate in him?—His crimes.
Every reply was temperate save one
And that was human when all's said and done :
The deposition, read to those who sit
In judgement on her, 'What has she to say?'
'Nothing, except that I succeeded in it.'

—You think that you have killed all Marats off?
—I think perhaps such men are now afraid.
The blade hung in its grooves. How should she know
The Terror still to come, as she was led
Red-smocked from gaol out into evening's red?
It was to have brought peace, that faultless blow.

Uncowed by the unimaginable result,
She loomed by in the cart beneath the eye
Of Danton, Desmoulins and Robespierre,
Heads in a rabble fecund in insult :
She had remade her calendar, called this
The Fourth Day of the Preparation of Peace.

Greater than Brutus was what Adam Lux
Demanded for her statue's sole inscription :
His pamphlet was heroic and absurd
And asked the privilege of dying too :
Though the republic raised to her no statue,
The brisk tribunal took him at his word.

What haunted that composure none could fault ?
For she, when shown the knife, had dropped her glance—
She 'who believed her death would raise up France'
As Chénier wrote who joined the later dead :
Her judge had asked : 'If you had gone uncaught,
Would you have then escaped ?' 'I would,' she said.

A daggered Virtue, Clio's roll of stone,
Action unsinewed into statuary !
Beneath that gaze what tremor was willed down ?
And, where the scaffold's shadow stretched its length,
What unlived life would struggle up against
Death died in the possession of such strength ?

Perhaps it was the memory of that cry
That cost her most as Catherine Marat
Broke off her testimony . . . But the blade
Inherited the future now and she
Entered a darkness where no irony
Seeps through to move the pity of her shade.

Note : Stanza 3 : Fouquier-Tinville was the public prosecutor.

4

MARAT DEAD
The Version of Jacques Louis David
*Citoyen, il suffit que je sois bien malheureuse
pour avoir droit à votre bienveillance.*
Charlotte Corday to Marat

They look like fact, the bath, the wall, the knife,
The splintered packing-case that served as table;
The linen could be priced by any housewife,
As could the weapon too, but not the sable
Suggestion here that colours all we feel
And animates this death-scene from the life
With red, brown, green reflections on the real.

Scaled back to such austerity, each tone
Now sensuous with sadness, would persuade
That in the calm the ugliness has gone
From the vast mouth and from the swaddled head;
And death that worked this metamorphosis
Has left behind no effigy of stone
But wrought an amorous languor with its kiss.

'Citizen, it is enough that I should be
A most unhappy woman to have right
To your benevolence' : the heeded plea
Lies on his desk, a patch of bloodied white,
Taking the eye beside the reddening bath,
And single-minded in duplicity,
Loud in the silence of this aftermath.

Words in this painting victimize us all :
Tyro or tyrant, neither shall evade
Such weapons : reader, you grow rational
And miss those sharp intentions that have preyed
On trusting literacy here : unmanned
By generosity and words you fall,
Sprawl forwards bleeding with your pen in hand.

She worked in blood, and paint absolves the man,
And in a bathtub laves all previous stains :
She is the dark and absence in the plan
And he a love of justice that remains.

5

Who was more deft, the painter or the girl?
Marat's best monument with this began,
That all her presence here's a truthless scrawl.

A SELF-PORTRAIT: DAVID

This is the face behind my face. You see
At every trembling touch of paint laid-in
To haunt the ground with shade, enough of me
To tell you what I am. This flesh puts by
The mind's imperious geometry,
The signature of will among the things
That will must change. From this day forth, distrust
Whatever I may do unless it show
A startled truth as in these eyes' misgivings,
These lips that, closed, confess 'I do not know.'

FOR DANTON

'Bound to the fierce Metropolis . . .'
The Prelude, Book X

In the autumn of 1793—the year in which he had instituted the
Revolutionary Tribunal—Danton went back to his birthplace, Arcis-
sur-Aube. After his return in November, he was to be arrested, tried
and condemned.

Who is the man that stands against this bridge
And thinks that he and not the river advances?
Can he not hear the links of consequence
Chiming his life away? Water is time.
Not yet, not yet. He fronts the parapet
Drinking the present with unguarded sense:

6

The stream comes on. Its music deafens him
To other sounds, to past and future wrong.
The beat is regular beneath that song.
He hears in it a pulse that is his own;
He hears the year autumnal and complete.
November waits for him who has not done

With seeings, savourings. Grape-harvest brings
The south into the north. This parapet
Carries him forward still, a ship from Rheims,
From where, in boyhood and on foot, he'd gone
'To see,' he said, 'the way a king is made',
The king that he himself was to uncrown—

Destroyed and superseded, then secure
In the possession of a perfect power
Returned to this : to river, town and plain,
Walked in the fields and knew what power he'd lost,
The cost to him of that metropolis where
He must come back to rule and Robespierre.

Not yet. This contrary perfection he
Must taste into a life he has no time
To live, a lingered, snatched maturity
Before he catches in the waterchime
The measure and the chain a death began,
And fate that loves the symmetry of rhyme
Will spring the trap whose teeth must have a man.

A BIOGRAPHY OF THE AUTHOR: A CENTO
Or what Rumour and History compounded
concerning the life of the late Sir John Denham
1615–69

He was born in Dublin, but two years later
before the Foggy Air of that Climate could influence
or any way adulterate his mind,
was brought from thence. Where he went to school
remains uncertain. At Oxford
he continued about three years, being looked upon
as a slow and dreaming young man
and given more to his cards and dice
than to study. After his refusing to pay a debt
to the college recorder and having told him
I never intended that
the President rattled him at a lecture in the chapell :
Thy father the judge he said *haz hanged*
many an honester man. It was at college
his love of gaming first manifested itself,
and when he had played away all his money
he would play away his father's wrought gold cappes.
At Lincoln's Inn he applied himself
to study the law. As good a student
as any in the house, he was not suspected
to be a witt. Yet he would game much and frequent
the company of gamesters, who rook'd him sometimes
of all he could wrap or get. Generally temperate
as to drink, one time having been merry,
a frolick comes into his head, and with a playsterer's brush
and a pott of inke, he blotted out
all the signes between Temple Barre and Charing-crosse
(this I had from R. Estcott esq. that carried the brush).
When his father objected to his gaming
he wrote, to prove his reformation
and to make sure of his patrimony, *The Anatomy of Play*,
a pamphlet exposing with lucidity
the evils of gaming. At four and twenty
he inherited on the death of the judge, 2 houses well furnished
and much plate, together with numerous estates
in four counties. These were sequestrated

because of his attachment to the king's party.
He aided in the escape of His Majesty, and also of the Duke of
   York—
a person he had much cause to regret later.
He remained faithful to the king
throughout imprisonment, spyings and embassies
between France and England, until
at the Restoration, Charles knighted him
because Denham had 'diverted the evil hour of my banishment'
with his verses. As Royal Surveyor
he knew nothing of architecture,
and would have set the Greenwich Palace
on piles at the very brink of the water. However,
he paved Holborn, being responsible
for the reformation of a thousand deformities in the streets,
the cure of noysom gutters
and the deobstruction of encounters. At fifty
'ancient and limping', he married for a second time. The match
was unequal in many respects, she being twenty-three
and beautiful and soon to become mistress
to the Duke of York. A year later he grew mad,
for having set out to see the free-stone quarries
at Portland in Dorset, he turned back
within a mile of them, and travelled to Hownslowe
to demand rents of the lands he had sold
many years before, thence to the king and told him
he was the Holy Ghost. The king
summoned Valentine Greatrakes, the Irish stroker
who stroked but could not cure him :
a diarist has him for dead, but emended that
to 'not yet dead, but distracted'.
His wife went into Somerset
travelling night and day to see him before he died
and if she could. Sir John was now stark mad
which was occasioned (as is said by some)
by the rough striking of Greatrakes upon his limbs
for they say that having taken the fluxing pills in Holland
and they not working, they rubbed his shins with mercury
but they supposed it lodged in the nerves
till the harsh strokes caused it to sublimate.
This was in April 1666 :
By September 'that great master of wit and reason'
no longer mad, but still noticeably eccentric,

9

has returned to Parliament, a member of various committees
and in regular attendance. My Lord Lisle writes :
'If he had not the name of being mad, I believe
in most companies he would be thought wittier
than ever he was. He has few extravagances besides that
of telling stories of himself, which he is always inclined to
and some of his acquaintances say that extreme vanity
was the cause of his madness, as it was the effect.'
There is little doubt that the cause of his madness
was youthful venery, but opinion attributed it
to his being a notorious cuckold at the hands
of the Duke of York, he going at noon-day with all his gentlemen
to visit my Lady Denham
in Scotland Yard, she declaring
she will not be his mistresse to go up and down the privy-stairs
but will be owned publicly; and so she is. Mr Evelyn
calls it bitchering, for the Duke of York
talks a little to her, and then she goes away,
and then he follows her again like a dog. In November
on the afternoon of the tenth
my Lady Denham is exceeding sick, even to death,
she saying and everyone else discoursing
that she is poysoned, but the physicians affirm
the cause of her sickness to have been
iliaca passio. At the turn of the year
my Lady Denham is at last dead,
but when the body was opened, the autopsy
revealed no trace of poison, though could not check
the persistence of contrary rumour, some
alleging it was administered in a cup of chocolate,
others that the Duchess of York had accomplished her death
with a powder of diamond, or that 'Old Denham'
being jealous and having no country house
to which he could carry his unfortunate wife
had made her travel a much longer journey
without stirring from London. The populace
had a design of tearing him in pieces
as soon as he should come abroad, but was appeased
by the magnificence of the funeral where he distributed
four times more burnt wine
than ever had been drunk at any burial in England—
soon afterwards, the Duchess of York
troubled with the appearance of the Lady Denham

10

bit off a piece of her tongue. Denham
in the ensuing quiet
and profiting by the remission of his disease
wrote one of his best pieces, the eulogy of Cowley,
but on account of his weakness
was forced to appoint Wren
Deputy Surveyor. He did not survive
his wife or his poem long, but died at his office
probably of an apoplexy
two years after her death. As to the disposition of his body
there was some hesitation :
What means this silence that may seeme to doome
Denham to an undistinguished tomb
wrote Mr Christopher Wase, but 'loath'd oblivion
and neglect' being averted, he was buried
in the Abbey.

LINES WRITTEN IN THE EUGANEAN HILLS

1

The tiles of the swimming pool are azure,
    Dyeing on breast and wings the swifts
That, transfigured, hunt its surface :
    This is man's landscape, all transfigurings
Across the thrust of origin—of rock
    Under schists and clays, their erratic
Contours cross-ruled by vine on vine :
    Over the table, flies are following-out the stains
Tasting the man-made, the mature stale wine.

2

An aridity haunts the edges of the fields :
    The irrigation jet, irising, arching
Across the cloud of its own wet smoke,
    Puts a gloss on the crop. But the cricket
Is raucous, the hoarse voice of that dust
    That whitening the grassroots of the burnt-out ditches,
Has webbed-over the spider's net with chalk.

11

3

Unshuttering vistas
mournfully the wizened
female custodian recites
snatches of Petrarch
whose statue cramped
in the cellarage gesticulates
beside his mummified cat, Laura.

4

D'Annunzio saw it all behind golden mist,
A wavering of decay, vegetable, vast,
That had taken hold on each statue, each relief,
And was eating and unmaking them, as if leaf by leaf.
Two wars, and the mathematic of the humanist
Re-declares itself in white persistence,
Slogans scaling the plinths and walls where Mao
And Lenin dispute the Palladian ratio.

DEATH IN VENICE

Glass gauds from Murano.
The band at Florian's are drowsing
drowned in the syrup of their rhapsody.
A high stack
flaring-off waste from Mestre
hangs beaconed across water
where each outboard's wake
is flexing, unmaking those marble
images, bridals of stone
and sea, restless to have
that piled longevity
down and done.

NEAR CORINIUM

The recalcitrance
                of whorl-wheel fossils
of belemnite teeth
                shatterings
from the meteors
                gods had hurled
according
        to those who also
lie in the subsoil these inlay :
                'I, Caius Martius restored
                this Jupiter column
                the Christians had defaced'
                                of which
only the limestone base . . .
                        those who,
these which—
                history's particles refusing
both completion
                and extinction :
traceries
        finer than the lines
of spider floss :
                it is as though
this torn tapestry
                faded calligraphy
were whole
        if only one could adjust
one's eyes to them :
                excavations
for the by-pass :
                the dust-motes turning like stars
which the air-currents lift

The glistening field has survived its battles :
   A fault in the window-pane takes hold,
Twists to a dip the plain of York :
   But at one shift of the eye the straight
Flows back to occupy that hollow,
   Shadows following ditch and field-line
In horizontals. It is no tyranny
   To the cycle a hedge hides and whose rider
Slotted into the scene, drifts by
   And, making the will of the land his own,
Is wing-swift land-bound. Birds alone
   Can seem to defy the law of the plain :
The lapwings shape out of nothing
   The fells they come dropping through; and their hills
Of air roll with the currents of a wind
   Calling to York from Jorvik as it tries
To speak through this casement where a fault in glass
   Keeps rippling and releasing tense horizons;
As if this place could be pried out of now,
   As if we could fly in the face of all we know.

CASAROLA
for Attilio Bertolucci

Cliffs come sheering down into woodland here :
   The trees—they are chestnuts—spread to a further drop
Where an arm of water rushes through unseen
   Still lost in leaves : you can hear it
Squandering its way towards the mill
   A path crossing a hillslope and a bridge
Leads to at last : the stones lie there
   Idle beside it : they were cut from the cliff
And the same stone rises in wall and roof
   Not of the mill alone, but of shed on shed
Whose mossed tiles like a city of the dead
   Grow green in the wood. There are no dead here

14

And the living no longer come
    In October to crop the trees : the chestnuts
Dropping, feed the roots they rose from :
    A rough shrine sanctifies the purposes
These doors once opened to, a desolation
    Of still-perfect masonry. There is a beauty
In this abandonment : there would be more
    In the slow activity of smoke
Seeping at roof and lintel; out of each low
    Unwindowed room rising to fill
Full with essences the winter wood
    As the racked crop dried. Waste
Is our way. An old man
    Has been gathering mushrooms. He pauses
To show his spoil, plumped by a soil
    Whose sweet flour goes unmilled :
Rapid and unintelligible, he thinks we follow
    As we feel for his invitations to yes and no :
Perhaps it's the mushrooms he's telling over
    Or this place that shaped his dialect, and where nature
Daily takes the distinctness from that signature
    Men had left there in stone and wood,
Among waning villages, above the cities of the plain.

PORTOBELLO CARNIVAL 1973

A malleability
                a precision
with which they keep the beat
                        their bodies
overflowing to the house-doors
                        dancing
so that the street
                is a jostled conduit
that contains them (just) :
                    the steel-band ride,
their pace decided
            by the crowd's pace

15

before their open truck
                              to a music
of detritus
              wheelhubs, cans :
the tempered oil-drums
                              yield a Caribbean sweetness
belied by the trumpet
                              that gliding on
ahead of the ostinato
                              divides
what the beat unites :
                              the trumpeter knows
and through his breath
                              and fingers the knowledge
flows into acid sound :
                              you will not go back
to the fronds, the sands
                              Windward, Leeward
and all those islands
                              the banner bears forward
under the promise
                      FOREVER :
below
        human peacocks and imaginary birds,
a devil
        hoisting as a flag
his black bat-wings
                              that have come unpinned (unpinioned) :
in all the sweat
                      and garish conglomeration of dress
there is a rightness
                      to every acrylic splash
spattering the London grey,
                              the unrelenting trumpet deriding
the drum-beat fable
                      of a tribal content
on this day of carnival,
                      the dissonance
half-assuaged in the sway of flesh
                              holding back time
dancing off history.

16

II PERFECTIONS

PROSE POEM
for John and Lisbeth

If objects are of two kinds—those
  That we contemplate and, the remainder, use,
I am unsure whether its poetry or prose
  First drew us to this jar. A century
Ago, an apothecary must have been its owner,
  Thankful that it was airtight. And in spite of time
It remains so still. Its cylinder of glass,
  Perfectly seamless, has the finality and satisfaction
Of the achieved act of an artisan. Indeed,
  The stopper of ground glass, that refused
To be freed from the containing neck,
  Was almost too well-made. What had to be done
If we were to undo it, was to pass
  A silk cord round the collar of glass
And rub it warm—but this friction
  Must be swift enough not to conduct its heat
Inside—the best protection against which
  (Only a third hand can ensure this feat)
Is a cube of ice on top of the stopper.
  Whether it was the rubbing only, or the warm
Grasp that must secure the bottle's body,
  The stopper, once more refusing at first,
Suddenly parted—breathed-out
  (So to speak) by the warmed expanding glass.
Remaining ice-cool itself, when
  Lightly oiled, it was now ready again
For use—but not before we had tried
  Jar against ear to find the sound inside it.
It gave off—no seashell murmur—
  A low, crystalline roar that wholly
Possessed one's cavities, a note (as it were)
  Of unfathomable distance—not emptiness,
For this dialogue between air and ear
  Was so full of electric imponderables, it could compare
Only with that molecular stealth when the jar
  Had breathed. There is one sole lack
Now that jar and stopper are in right relation—
  An identifiable aroma : what we must do
Is to fill it with coffee, for use, scent and contemplation.

19

DEPARTURE

You were to leave and being all but gone,
   Turned on yourselves, to see that stream
Which bestows a flowing benediction and a name
   On our house of stone. Late, you had time
For a glance, no more, to renew your sense
   Of how the brook—in spate now—
Entered the garden, pooling, then pushing
   Over a fall, to sidle a rock or two
Before it was through the confine. Today,
   The trail of your jet is scoring the zenith
Somewhere, and I, by the brink once more,
   Can tell you now what I had to say
But didn't then : it is here
   That I like best, where the waters disappear
Under the bridge-arch, shelving through coolness,
   Thought, halted at an image of perfection
Between gloom and gold, in momentary
   Stay, place of perpetual threshold,
Before all flashes out again and on
   Tasseling and torn, reflecting nothing but sun.

IMAGES OF PERFECTION

            . . . What do we see
   In the perfect thing ? Is our seeing
Merely a measuring, a satisfaction
   To be compared ? How do we know at sight
And for what they are, these rarenesses
   That are right ? In yesterday's sky
Every variety of cloud accompanied earth,
   Mares' tails riding past mountainous anvils,
While their shadows expunged our own :
   It was pure display—all a sky could put on
In a single day, and yet remain sky.
   I mean, you felt in the air the sway
Of sudden apocalypse, complete revelation :

20

But what it came to was a lingering
At the edge of time, a perfect neighbouring,
　　Until the twilight brought it consummation,
Seeping in violet through the entire scene.
　　Where was the meaning, then? Did Eden
Greet us ungated? Or was that marrying
　　Purely imaginary and, if it were,
What do we see in the perfect thing?

RHYMES

Perfect is the word I can never hear
　　Without a sensation as of seeing—
As though a place should grow perfectly clear,
　　The light on the look of it agreeing
To show—not all there is to be seen,
　　But all you would wish to know
At a given time. Word and world rhyme
　　As the penstrokes might if you drew
The spaciousness reaching down through a valley view,
　　Gathering the lines into its distances
As if they were streams, as if they were eye-beams:
　　Perfect, then, the eye's command in its riding,
Perfect the coping hand, the hillslopes
　　Drawing it into such sight the sight would miss,
Guiding the glance the way perfection is.

THE PERFECTION

There is that moment when,
the sun almost gone,
red gains and deepens on
neighbouring cloud :

21

and the shadows that seam
and grain it take
to themselves
indelible black :

yet we never know it
until it has been
for the moment it is
and the next has brought in

a lost pitch,
a lack-lustre pause
in the going glow
where the perfection was.

III SEASONS

THE HESITATION

Spring lingers-out its arrival in these woods :
    A generation of flowers has been and gone
Before one tree has put on half its leaves :
    A butterfly wavers into flight yet scarcely wakes :
Chill currents of the air it tries to ride
    Cannot fulfill the promises of the sun
To favoured coverts sheltered beneath a hillside :
    Is it may-blossom smokes on the thicket crest,
Or the pallor of hoar-frost whitening its last ?

THE FARING

That day, the house was so much a ship
    Clasped by the wind, the whole sky
Piling its cloud-wrack past,
    To be sure you were on dry land
You must go out and stand in that stream
    Of air : the entire world out there
Was travelling too : in each gap the tides
    Of space felt for the earth's ship sides :
Over fields, new-turned, the cry
    And scattered constellations of the gulls
Were messengers from that unending sea, the sky :
    White on brown, a double lambency
Pulsed, played where the birds, intent
    On nothing more than the ploughland's nourishment,
Brought the immeasurable in : wing on wing
    Taking new lustres from the turning year
Above seasonable fields, they tacked and climbed
    With a planet's travelling, rhymed here with elsewhere
In the sea-salt freshnesses of tint and air.

THE METAMORPHOSIS

Bluebells come crowding a fellside
    A stream once veined. It rises
Like water again where, bell on bell,
    They flow through its bed, each rope
And rivulet, each tributary thread
    Found-out by flowers. And not the slope
Alone, runs with this imaginary water :
    Marshes and pools of it stay
On the valley-floor, fed (so the eye would say)
    From the same store and streamhead.
Like water, too, this blueness not all blue
    Goes ravelled with groundshades, grass and stem,
As the wind dishevels and strokes it open;
    So that the mind, in salutory confusion,
Surrendering up its powers to the illusion,
    Could, swimming in metamorphoses, believe
Water itself might move like a flowing of flowers.

BELOW TINTERN

The river's mirrorings remake a world
    Green to the cliff-tops, hanging
Wood by wood, towards its counterpart :
    Green gathers there as no green could
That water did not densen. Yet why should mind
    So eagerly swim down and through
Such towering dimness? Because that world seems true?
    And yet it could not, if it were,
Suspend more solid castles in the air.
    Machicolations, look-outs for mind's eye
Feed and free it with mere virtuality
    Where the images elude us. For they are true enough
Set wide with invitation where they lie
    Those liquid thresholds, that inverted sky
Gripped beneath rockseams by the valley verdure,
    Lost to reflection as the car bends by.

PROVIDENCE

It is May : 'A bad winter,'
   They prophesy, the old women—they
Who remember still—for I cannot—
   Years when the hawthorns were as thick as now :
Spray on spray hangs over
   In heavy flounces, white swags
Weigh down the pliancy of branches,
   Drag at a whole tree until it bends :
I thought it must be these snow-brides, snow-ghosts
   Brought-on their unseasonable dream of frosts :
But old women know the blossoms must give way
   To berry after berry, as profuse as they,
On which, come winter, the birds will feed :
   For what in the world could justify and bring
Inexplicable plenty if not the birds' need ?—
   And winter must be harsh for appetite
Such as they have the means now to requite :
   Old women reason providentially
From other seasons, remembering how
   Winter set out to hunt the sparrows down
In years when the hawthorns were as thick as now.

MUSHROOMS
for Jon and Jill

Eyeing the grass for mushrooms, you will find
A stone or stain, a dandelion puff
Deceive your eyes—their colour is enough
To plump the image out to mushroom size
And lead you through illusion to a rind
That's true—flint, fleck or feather. With no haste
Scent-out the earthy musk, the firm moist white,
And, played-with rather than deluded, waste
None of the sleights of seeing : taste the sight
You gaze unsure of—a resemblance, too,

27

Is real and all its likes and links stay true
To the weft of seeing. You, to begin with,
May be taken in, taken beyond, that is,
This place of chiaroscuro that seemed clear,
For realer than a myth of clarities
Are the meanings that you read and are not there :
Soon, in the twilight coolness, you will come
To the circle that you seek and, one by one,
Stooping into their fragrance, break and gather,
Your way a winding where the rest lead on
Like stepping stones across a grass of water.

IN THE INTENSITY OF FINAL LIGHT

In the intensity of final light
   Deepening, dyeing, moss on the tree-trunks
Glares more green than the foliage they bear :
   Hills, then, have a way of taking fire
To themselves as though they meant to hold
   In a perpetuity of umber, amber, gold
Those forms that, by the unstable light of day,
   Refuse all final outline, drift
From a dew-cold blue into green-shot grey :
   In the intensity of final light
A time of loomings, then a chime of lapses
   Failing from woodslopes, summits, sky,
Leaving, for the moonrise to untarnish,
   Hazed airy fastnesses where the last rays vanish.

THE SPRING SYMPHONY

This is the Spring Symphony. Schumann
   Wrote it in autumn. Now it is June.
Nothing to deny, nothing to identify
   The season of this music. Autumn in the cellos

Is proverbial, yet these consent
   To be the perfect accompaniment to such a day
As now declares itself : on the flexed grass
   New sheen : the breeze races in it
Blent with light as on the face of waters :
   The returning theme—new earth, new sky—
Filled the orchestral universe until,
   On fire to be fleshed-out, leaf and seed
Became their dream and dazzle in freshness still :
   Yet, self-consuming, these
Emanations, energies that press
   In light and wind to their completeness,
Seem half irate : invaded by this music
   The summer's single theme might be
The mind's own rage against mortality
   In wasting, hastening flight towards
The sum of all, the having done.
   This summer sound is the Spring Symphony
Written in autumn. Death is its ground,
   Life hurrying to death, its urgency,
Its timelessness, its melody and wound.

NATURE POEM

This August heat, this momentary breeze,
First filtering through, and then prolonged in it,
Until you feel the two as one, this sound
Of water that is sound of leaves, they all
In stirrings and comminglings so recall
The ways a poem flows, they ask to be
Written into a permanence—not stilled
But given pulse and voice. So many shades,
So many filled recesses, stones unseen
And daylight darknesses beneath the trees,
No single reading renders up complete
Their shifting text—a poem, too, in this,
They bring the mind half way to its defeat,
Eluding and exceeding the place it guesses,
Among these overlappings, half-lights, depths,
The currents of this air, these hiddenesses.

THE WHIP

We are too much on the outside
in the inside of the ear
to sort clear at first
the unrolling of the thunder : then
deserting the distances, all
that sunken mumbling turns
to a spine of sound, a celestial
whipline, the crack at the end
of each lash implied under the first
spreading salvo the ears
had been merely fumbling with :
one sky-track now
flashes through them as keen
as the lightning dancing to the eye
the shape of the whip that woke
in them its uncoiling soundscape.

TO SEE THE HERON

To see the heron rise
detaching blue from the blue
that, smoking, lies along
field-hollows, shadowings
of humidity : to see it
set off that blaze
where ranks of autumn trees
are waiting just for this
raised torch, this touch,
this leisurely sideways
wandering ascension to unite
their various brightnesses, their fire-
music as a voice might
riding sound : risen
it is darkening now
against the sullen sky blue,
so let it go

unaccompanied save by the thought
that this is autumn and the stream
whose course its eye is travelling
the source of fish : to see the heron
hang wondering where
to stoop, to alight and strike.

ONE DAY OF AUTUMN

One day of autumn
sun had uncongealed
the frost that clung
wherever shadows spread
their arctic greys among
October grass : mid-
field an oak still
held its foliage intact
but then began
releasing leaf by leaf
full half,
till like a startled
flock they scattered
on the wind : and one
more venturesome than all
the others shone far out
a moment in mid-air,
before it glittered off
and sheered into the dip
a stream ran through
to disappear with it

OCTOBER

Autumn seems ending : there is lassitude
Wherever ripeness has not filled its brood
Of rinds and rounds : all promises are fleshed
Or now they fail. Far gone, these blackberries—
For each one that you pull, two others fall
Full of themselves, the leaves slick with their ooze :
Awaiting cold, we welcome in the frost
To cleanse these purples, this discandying,
As eagerly as we shall look to spring.

OLD MAN'S BEARD

What we failed to see
was twines of the wild clematis
climbing all summer
through each burdened tree :

not till the leaves were gone
did we begin to take
the measure of what strength
had fed from the limestone

that roof of feathered seed
bearding the woods now
in its snowy foliage
yet before fall of snow

and what silent cordage bound
the galaxy together where
December light reflected
from star on hairy star

innumerably united
in a cascade, a cloud, a wing
to hang their canopy above
the roots they were strangling.

. . . OR TRAVELLER'S JOY

I return late
on a wintry road : the beam
has suddenly lit
flowers of frost, or so they seem :

Traveller's Joy ! the recognition
flares as soon, almost,
as the headlights quit
those ghosts of petals :

a time returns, when men
fronting the winter starkness
were travellers travailing
against hail, mud, dark :

then, whoever it was,
much road behind him,
coming, perhaps, at dawn
with little to remind him

he was cared for, kinned,
saw from the road
the hedgerow loaded
and thought it rimed :

and so it was : the name
he drew from that sudden brightness
came as if his joy
were nature's, too :

and the sweet illusion
persists with the name
into present night,
under the travelling beam.

The cold came. It has photographed the scene
With so exact a care, that you can look
From field-white and from wood-black to the air
Now that the snow has ceased, and catch no shade
Except these three—the third is the sky's grey :
Will it thicken or thaw, this rawness menacing?
The sky stirs : the sky refuses to say :
But it lets new colour in : its thinning smoke
Opens towards a region beyond snow,
Rifts to a blueness rather than a blue :
Brought to a sway, the whole day hesitates
Through the sky of afternoon, and you beneath,
As if questions of weather were of life and death.

IV BAGATELLES

THE DEATH OF WILL

The end was more of a melting :
as if frost turned heavily to dew
and the flags, dragged down by it,
clung to their poles : marble becoming glue.

Alive, no one had much cared
for Will : Will no sooner gone,
there was a *je ne sais quoi*, a *ton*
'fell from the air' :

And how strange that, Will once dead,
Passion must die, too,
although they'd had nothing to do
with each other, so it was said :

It was then everyone stopped looking
for the roots of decay,
for curative spears and chapels perilous
and the etymology of 'heyday' :

Parents supine, directionless,
looked to their wilful children now :
was this metempsychosis?
was Will reborn in them somehow?

Someone should record Will's story.
Someone should write a book on *Will and Zen*.
Someone should trace all those who
knew Will, to interview them. Someone

When the old servant reveals she is the mother
    Of the young count whose elder brother
Has betrayed him, the heroine, disguised
    As the Duke's own equerry, sings *Or'*
Che sono, pale from the wound she has received
    In the first act. The entire court
Realise what has in fact occurred and wordlessly
    The waltz song is to be heard now
In the full orchestra. And we, too,
    Recall that meeting of Marietta with the count
Outside the cloister in Toledo. She faints :
    Her doublet being undone, they find
She still has on the hair-shirt
    Worn ever since she was a nun
In Spain. So her secret is plainly out
    And Boccaleone (blind valet
To the Duke) confesses it is he *(Or'son'io)*
    Who overheard the plot to kidnap the dead
Count Bellafonte, to burn by night
    The high camp of the gipsy king
Alfiero, and by this stratagem quite prevent
    The union of both pairs of lovers.
Now the whole cast packs the stage
    Raging in chorus round the quartet—led
By Alfiero (having shed his late disguise)
    And Boccaleone (shock has restored his eyes) :
Marietta, at the first note from the count
    (Long thought dead, but finally revealed
As Alfiero), rouses herself, her life
    Hanging by a thread of song, and the Duke,
Descending from his carriage to join in,
    Dispenses pardon, punishment and marriage.
Exeunt to the Grand March, Marietta
    (Though feebly) marching, too, for this
Is the 'Paris' version where we miss
    The ultimate dénouement when at the command
Of the heroine *(Pura non son')* Bellafonte marries
    The daughter of the gipsy king and

IN THE STUDIO
for Fraser Steel

'Recorded ambience'—this
is what they call
silences put back
between the sounds :
leaves might fall
on to the roof-glass to compound
an instant ambience
from the drift of sibilants :
but winter boughs
cannot enter—they
distort like weed
under the glass water :
this (sifted) silence
now recording (one
minute only of it)
comprises what
you did not hear before
you began to listen—
the sighs that
in a giant building
rise up trapped between
its sound-proofed surfaces
murmuring, replying
to themselves, gathering
power like static
from the atmosphere : you do
hear this ambience?
it rings true : for silence
is an imagined thing.

MISPRINT
for L. S. Dembo

'Meeting' was what
I had intended :
'melting' ended
an argument that
should have led
out (as it were)
into a clearing, an
amphitheatre
civic or sylvan
where what could not be
encompassed stood
firmly encompassing
column on column, tree on tree
in their clear ring :
there I had hoped to come
into my true
if transitory kingdom :
instead, one
single letter has un-
made, punned
meaning away into
a statuary circle
becoming snow
and down I dissolve with it
statue on statue
gobbet on slithering gobbet

MAINTENANT
for Samuel Menashe

Hand
holding on to this
instant metamorphosis,
the syllables maintain
against the lapse
of time that they remain
here, where all else escapes

40

SKY WRITING

A plane goes by,
and the sky takes hold
on the frail, high chalk-line
of its vapour-trail, picks
it apart, combs out
and spreads the filaments
down either side
the spine of a giant plume
which rides written on air now :
that flocculent, unwieldy sceptre
begins its sway with
an essential uncertainty, a
veiled threat tottering it
slowly to ruin, and the sky
grasping its tatters
teases them thin,
letting in blue until,
all flaxen cobblings, lit
transparencies, they
give up their ghosts
to air, lost in their opposite.

INTO DISTANCE

Swift cloud
across still cloud
drifting east
so that the still
seems also on the move
the other way : a vast
opposition throughout the sky
and, as one stands
watching the separating
gauzes, greys, the eyes

41

wince dizzily away from them :
feeling for roots anew
one senses the strength
in planted legs, the pull
at neck, tilted
upwards to a blue that
ridding itself of all
its drift keeps now
only those few, still
island clouds to occupy
its oceanic spread
where a single, glinting plane
bound on and over
is spinning into distance and ahead
of its own sound

EMBASSY

A breeze keeps fleshing the flag :
   I watch it droop, then reassemble
On air an emblem I do not know :
   Nor does that woman know the part
She plays in this rhymescheme that no art
   Has prompted : for the breeze begins
Feeling along the dyed silk of her hair,
   Unfurling its viking platinum to the same
Rhythm with which the flag bursts into flame :
   Steam seeps from a manhole in the asphalt :
And that, too, leans to the common current,
   Goes upward taking shape from the unseen
In this unpremeditable action where
   A wind is having its way with all swayable things,
Combing through flag and steam, streaming-out hair.

THE RACE

These waters run secretively until
   Rushing the race where a mill stood once
The weight comes drumming down,
   Crushing-out whiteness as they fall
And fill with a rocking yeast this pool
   They clamour across : clamour and clamber
Blindly till again they find their leat
   And level, narrow-out into
A now-smooth riverlane and pouring on
   Go gathering up the silence where they run.

V IN ARDEN

IN ARDEN
'This is the forest of Arden . . .'

Arden is not Eden, but Eden's rhyme :
  Time spent in Arden is time at risk
And place, also : for Arden lies under threat :
  Ownership will get what it can for Arden's trees :
No acreage of green-belt complacencies
  Can keep Macadam out : Eden lies guarded :
Pardonable Adam, denied its gate,
  Walks the grass in a less-than-Eden light
And whiteness that shines from a stone burns with his fate :
  Sun is tautening the field's edge shadowline
Along the wood beyond : but the contraries
  Of this place are contrarily unclear :
A haze beats back the summer sheen
  Into a chiaroscuro of the heat :
The down on the seeded grass that beards
  Each rise where it meets with sky,
Ripples a gentle fume : a fine
  Incense, smelling of hay smokes by :
Adam in Arden tastes its replenishings :
  Through its dense heats the depths of Arden's springs
Convey echoic waters—voices
  Of the place that rises through this place,
Overflowing, as it brims its surfaces
  In runes and hidden rhymes, in chords and keys
Where Adam, Eden, Arden run together
  And time itself must beat to the cadence of this river.

THE ROE DEER

We must anticipate the dawn one day,
Crossing the long field silently to see
The roe deer feed. Should there be snow this year
Taking their tracks, searching their colours out,

47

The dusk may help us to forestall their doubt
And drink the quiet of their secrecy
Before, the first light lengthening, they are gone.
One day we must anticipate the dawn.

THE SHAFT
for Guy Davenport

The shaft seemed like a place of sacrifice :
    You climbed where spoil heaps from the hill
Spilled out into a wood, the slate
    Tinkling underfoot like shards, and then
You bent to enter : a passageway :
    Cervix of stone : the tick of waterdrops,
A clear clepsydra : and squeezing through
    Emerged into cathedral space, held-up
By a single rocksheaf, a gerbe
    Buttressing-back the roof. The shaft
Opened beneath it, all its levels
    Lost in a hundred feet of water.
Those miners—dust, beards, mattocks—
    They photographed seventy years ago,
Might well have gone to ground here, pharoahs
    Awaiting excavation, their drowned equipment
Laid-out beside them. All you could see
    Was rock reflections tunneling the floor
That water covered, a vertical unfathomed,
    A vertigo that dropped through centuries
To the first who broke into these fells :
    The shaft was not a place to stare into
Or not for long : the adit you entered by
    Filtered a leaf-light, a phosphorescence,
Doubled by water to a tremulous fire
    And signalling you back to the moist door
Into whose darkness you had turned aside
    Out of the sun of an unfinished summer.

DE SOLE : after Ficino
for *Homero Aridjis*

If once a year
the house of the dead
stood open
and those dwelling
under its roof
were shown the world's
great wonders, all
would marvel beyond every other thing at
the sun

MACDUFF

This wet sack, wavering slackness
   They drew out silent through the long
Blood-edged incision, this black
   Unbreathing thing they must first
Hoist from a beam by its heels and swing
   To see whether it could yet expel
Death through each slimy nostril,
   This despaired-of, half-born mishap
Shuddered into a live calf, knew
   At a glance mother, udder and what it must do
Next and did it, mouthing for milk.
   The cow, too, her womb stitched back inside,
Her hide laced up, leans down untaught
   To lick clean her untimely firstborn :
'Pity it's a male.' She looms there innocent
   That words have meanings, but long ago
This blunt lapsarian instinct, poetry,
   Found life's sharpest, readiest
Rhyme, unhesitating—it was knife—
   By some farm-yard gate, perhaps,
That led back from nature into history.

TREE

I took a tree for a guide—I mean
   Gazing sideways, I had chosen idly
Over walls, fields and other trees,
   This single elm, or it had chosen me :
At all events, it so held my mind,
   I did not stop to admire as otherwise I should
The charlock all in yellow fire against
   A sky of thunder-grey : I walked on,
Taking my bearings from that trunk
   And, as I moved, the tree moved too
Alongside, or it seemed to do. Seemed?
   Incontrovertibly the intervening hedgerows occupied
Their proper place, a mid-ground
   In a bounded scene, myopically vague
At each extremity. But the elm
   Paced as if parallel for half a mile
Before I could outstrip it and consign
   The sight into the distances. A trick
Of the eye no doubt, but one not easily
   Put out of mind : that branch-crowned tower,
That stalking memorial of Dunsinane
   Reared alien there, but it was I
Was the stranger on that silent field,
   Gazing unguarded, guideless at a frontier
I could never cross nor whose image raze.

THE GAP

It could be that you are driving by.
   You do not need the whole of an eye
To command the thing : the edge
   Of a merely desultory look
Will take it in—it is a gap
   (No more) where you'd expect to see
A field-gate, and there well may be

But it is flung wide, and the land so lies
All you see is space—that, and the wall
   That climbs up to the spot two ways
To embrace absence, frame skies :
   Why does one welcome the gateless gap?
As an image to be filled with the meaning
   It doesn't yet have? As a confine gone?
A saving grace in so much certainty of stone?
   Reason can follow reason, one by one.
But the moment itself, abrupt
   With the pure surprise of seeing,
Will outlast all after-knowledge and its map—
   Even, and perhaps most then, should the unseen
Gate swing-to across that gap.

THE SCREAM

Night. A dream so drowned my mind,
   Slowly it rose towards that sound,
Hearing no scream in it, but a high
   Thin note, such as wasp or fly
Whines-out when spider comes dancing down
   To inspect its net. Curtains—
I dragged them back—muffled the cry :
   It rang in the room, but I could find
No web, wasp, fly. Blackly
   Beyond the pane, the same sound
Met the ear and, whichever way
   You pried for its source, seemed to be everywhere.
Torch, stair, door : the black
   Was wavering in the first suffusion
Of the small hours' light. But nothing
   Came clearly out of that obscure
Past-midnight, unshaped world, except
   The shrill of this savaging. I struck uphill
And, caught in the torchbeam, saw
   A lustre of eye, a dazzle on tooth
And stripe : badger above its prey

51

Glared worrying at that strident thing
It could neither kill nor silence. It swung
    Round to confront the light and me,
Sinewed, it seemed, for the attack, until
    I flung at it, stoned it back
And away from whatever it was that still
    Screamed on, hidden in greyness. A dream
Had delivered me to this, and a dream
    Once more seemed to possess one's mind,
For light could not find an embodiment for that scream,
    Though it found the very spot and tussock
That relentlessly breathed and heaved it forth.
    Was it a sound half-underground? Would badger
Bury its prey? Thoughts like these
    No thoughts at all, crowded together
To appall the mind with dream uncertainties.
    I flashed at the spot. It took reason
To unknot the ravel that hindered thought,
    And reason could distinguish what was there,
But could no more bear the cry
    Than the untaught ear. It was the tussock lived
And turned, now, at the touch of sight
    —You could eye the lice among its spines—
To a hedgehog. Terrible in the denial
    Of all comfort, it howled on here
For the lease that was granted it, the life
    That was safe, and which it could not feel
Was its own yet. It howled down death
    So that death might meet with its equal
Ten times the size of the despised life
    It had hunted for. In this comedy
Under the high night, this refusal
    To die with a taciturn, final dignity
A wolf's death, the scream
    In its nest of fleas took on the sky.

TRANSLATING THE BIRDS

The buzzard's two-note cry falls plaintively,
   And, like a seabird's, hesitates between
A mewing, a regret, a plangent plea,
   Or so we must translate it who have never
Hung with the buzzard or above the sea.

It veers a haughty circle with sun-caught breast :
   The small birds are all consternation now,
And do not linger to admire the sight,
   The flash of empery that solar fire
Lends to the predatory ease of flight.

The small birds have all taken to the trees,
   Their eyes alert, their garrulousness gone :
Beauty does not stir them, realists to a man,
   They know what awe's exacted by a king,
They know that now is not the time to sing.

They'll find their way back into song once more
   Who've only sung in metaphor and we
Will credit them with arias, minstrelsy,
   And, eager always for the intelligible,
Instruct those throats what meanings they must tell.

But supply pulsing, wings against the air,
   With yelp that bids the silence of small birds,
Now it is the buzzard owns the sky
   Thrusting itself beyond the clasp of words,
Word to dance with, dally and outfly.

THE SCAR

That night, the great tree split
   Where it forked, and a full half lay
At morning, prone by the other
   To await decay. The scar
Of cleavage gleams along the trunk
   With such a tall and final whiteness,
It is the living tree seems dead
   That rears from its own done life
Preparing to put on leaf. Buds
   Bead and soon the leaves will cover
That sapless-seeming wintershape all over.
   A debris clings there and claws
At the tree-foot, spills out
   Up half a hill in bone-white antlerings :
Over it all, the scar glints down,
   And a spring light pulsating ashen,
You would swear that through the shuddered trunk
   Still tremors the memory of its separation.

AT DAWN
in memoriam F.M.D.

The blue took you, a wing of ash :
   Returning from the summit where
We had released you into the sky
   And air of earliest day, we saw
Deer at gaze, deer drinking
   Before the blaze of desert sun
Dispersed them : that liquid look
   So held us, it was less a thing
Consolatory than a fact of morning,
   Its freshness returning us to time,
Its farness acknowledging the claim
   Of such distance as we shall only know
On a wing of ash, absorbed against the blue.